VICTORIAN CHILDREN

Eleanor Allen

Adam & Charles Black

London

BLACK'S JUNIOR REFERENCE BOOKS
General editor R. J. Unstead

Published by A & C Black (Publishers) Limited
35 Bedford Row, London WC1R 4JH

ISBN 0 7136 1324 6

© 1973 A & C Black (Publishers) Ltd
First published 1973
Reprinted 1979, 1983

Filmset and printed in Great Britain by BAS Printers Limited,
Over Wallop, Hampshire

Contents

ACKNOWLEDGEMENTS

The author and publishers are grateful to the following for permission to reproduce illustrations: Mary Evans Picture Library, 32b, 40, 41, 42a & b, 45, 50, 52, 61, 62a; Mansell Collection, 7a, 11a & b, 13, 18b, 19, 20b, 22, 23, 25, 27a & b, 28a, 33, 34, 36, 37a, 38, 48, 49, 54, 55, 56, 57, 59, cover and endpapers; Radio Times Hulton Picture Library, 4, 6, 7b, 8, 9, 10a & b, 12a, b & c, 14, 15, 16, 18a, 20a, 21a & b, 24b, 28b, 29, 30, 31, 32a, 35, 37b, 39, 42c, 43, 44, 46, 47, 51, 53, 58, 60, 62b, 63; Gwen Young, 24a, 26.

The line drawings are by G. R. Allen.

HOME SWEET HOME

What did Victorian Children Wear?

 ueen Victoria's reign was over sixty years long and fashions changed almost as rapidly as they do today. Here you can see only a few of the more interesting fashions that you might have worn as a well-to-do child, at different times in the period.

As a boy in the 1850s you might have looked something like the boy below on the left. This was the first time boys had ever worn short trousers which showed their knees.

In the 1860s you would have tried to look as grown up as possible in a tweed suit made by your father's tailor. A big floppy bow and bowler hat completed the outfit.

The sailor suit was popular at various times during the Queen's reign and was possibly one of the few fashions that were approved of by the boys as well as by their parents. The suit was made of blue serge and the hat bore the name of a ship in gold braid.

*A boy's suit
in the 1850s.*

*The popular
sailor suit.*

A Norfolk suit.

The Fauntleroy suit, 1888.

The suit on the left was popular in the 1880s. It was called the Norfolk suit. Again, it was a cut down version of a man's suit. The trousers were called knickerbockers and were made of the same tweed-like material as the jacket. It aimed at a casual effect, but this was somewhat spoilt by the stiff white collar and tie.

Baby's costume advertised in 1887.

The silliest fashion ever designed for boys was probably the Fauntleroy suit. In it you would have tried to look like a cavalier from the reign of Charles I. These suits got their name from the central character in a book called *Little Lord Fauntleroy*. The suit was made of velvet with a big collar of white lace. To add to the 'romantic' effect you would have worn your hair shoulder length. This was definitely not a suitable outfit for climbing trees!

Despite the petticoats, the child on the left is a boy. Little boys were kept in dresses with girlish underwear until the age of four and their hair was kept long too. When they were *breeched* (allowed to wear trousers) they felt very grown-up indeed.

In the 1840s a girl's knickers were intended to be seen.
They were called pantalettes and ended just below the
knee with a row of frills.

These ladies on their picnic are wearing
very wide dresses, supported by a frame of
steel called a crinoline. Girls in crinolines
had to be very careful how they moved about
a room, in case they knocked things over.

Alice in Wonderland was a very popular book
in Victoria's reign and for a time girls were
dressed in the familiar style of Alice. They
wore short crinolines, pantalettes just peep-
ing, and strapped shoes. Their hair hung
loose instead of in a net as it had been with
the crinoline.

*Short crinoline
with pantalettes.*

The bustle.

In summer poor children went barefoot. In winter they wore clogs or rough boots.

The bustle was a very odd fashion. It appeared in the late 1870s. As you see, girls wore rows of frills down the back of their skirt, or the skirt was bunched up and decorated with a big bow on the bottom. Sitting down must have been quite a problem.

There were no special clothes for play. Children were expected to play 'properly' and not make their hat and gloves dirty. Imagine playing in some of these clothes! Victorian children managed to enjoy themselves, though they must have been uncomfortable, especially in hot weather.

Poorer class children did not have the same problems. Instead of being over-dressed, they did not wear enough clothes. Generally they wore no underclothing. Their outer clothes were often little better than rags, having been bought second- or even third-hand.

Toys and Entertainment

hildren in Victoria's reign had no radios, television sets or record players to entertain them, Now, a hundred years or so later, you probably find it difficult to imagine what life was like without these things, and wonder what the children did to pass their time.

NURSERY TOYS

The younger children of well-to-do parents had nurseries stocked with lots of beautiful toys, though there was not such a great variety as there is today.

In most nurseries the favourite was the rocking horse. He was a dashing but sturdy creature made of wood and gaily painted. The finest sort was a very realistic dapple grey with a mane of real horse hair.

A toyshop in 1895.

Perhaps the second in nursery popularity with the girls was the dolls' house. This was a toy which mothers approved of because girls could learn from it how to run a home properly. By the 1880s furniture for dolls' houses was being made in perfect detail.

Even small objects such as lamps, ornaments, and libraries of books could be bought. The walls and floors were decorated in the fashion of the times.

Boys preferred something a little more adventurous. They chose boxes of tin or lead soldiers in bright regimental uniforms. These were often collected for their uniforms as much as for fighting mock battles, though toy forts and cannon were available for those who wanted them. Winston Churchill, as a boy, was fond of planning battles with his collection of soldiers.

Clockwork trains became popular in the later part of the period, as the railways themselves developed. The oldest known toy train of any sort in England dates from about 1840 and had to be pushed along its straight, tree-lined track.

Toy engine with a flywheel friction drive, 1840.

The dolls of Victoria's reign were, perhaps, the most beautiful ever made. It was the great age of the wax and china doll, though only the head and shoulders were made of these materials—the body would be made of stuffed calico, kid, or wood.

Most dolls of the period were dressed as grown-ups. Their gorgeous clothes were made of such rich fabrics as satin, taffeta, or lace. They were sewn by hand with the greatest care. Care was also taken to give the dolls different expressions so that no two dolls looked alike. Sometimes they had real human hair.

A popular doll of 1889.

Girl on a tricycle, 1870.

The Victorians loved novelty and experimented with walking, talking and sleeping dolls. They even introduced an eating doll which could be fed on sweets which reappeared out of its foot!

Obviously, these dolls were very expensive and were easily broken. Some mothers bought dolls of waxed rubber for their children or wooden dolls with jointed limbs, called Dutch dolls, which did not cost so much.

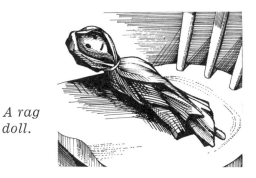

A rag doll.

A poor girl might have longed for these dolls in shop windows, but she would never have owned any of them. Instead she might have a rag doll. Sometimes she made one herself, out of a wooden spoon and a piece of cloth.

Nursery games were similar to the ones played today. But because parents liked the games to be 'improving' they usually had an instructive picture or message. Children played with jig-saw puzzles, draughts and cards.

Clockwork toys, wound up with a key so that their legs moved.

A sheet of 'twopence coloured'.

PASTIMES FOR OLDER CHILDREN

Older children, especially boys, enjoyed owning a toy theatre. They spent many happy hours and a lot of pocket money on preparing their plays.

First they had to buy a stage. This was usually made of wood and cardboard with a row of tin footlights along the front. The footlights had oil-burning wicks which flickered in blue, green or amber. If a draught caught them there was a risk of the whole theatre burning down!

Sheets of characters and scenes cost a penny plain or twopence ready coloured. Most children preferred to do the colouring themselves—it was part of the pleasure. They coloured in the characters, then cut them out and glued them on to cardboard.

Plays for the toy theatre usually had fighting or battle scenes in them, as you can tell from the titles— *The Blood-red Knight*, *The Battle of Waterloo* and *Rob Roy*.

Older children and adults enjoyed buying pictures of famous actors and actresses and sticking little tinsel dots on to their costumes until the picture glittered with bright points of light. It would then be put in a mahogany frame and kept on the mantelpiece.

Perhaps these hobbies may seem rather tame to us nowadays, but we must remember that these children had never watched plays on television, and few of them had visited a real theatre. They had to create their own excitement.

Theatres still had a bad name from earlier in the century, when they were uncomfortable and rowdy places, but there was one respectable theatre to which parents could take their children. It was called Astley's. There the family could enjoy exciting plays called melodramas and watch circus acts. But for many children their first experience of a real theatre was a pantomime at Christmas.

A family party at the pantomime, Drury Lane, 1870.

While their brothers prepared plays, the older girls were busy with their needlework. They practised their stitches by embroidering letters of the alphabet, texts or complicated landscapes with trees, flowers and animals inside a fancy border. These pieces of embroidery, which were very skilfully done, were called *samplers*. A girl might spend anything from several months to several years on sewing a sampler.

After she had finished her sampler she might embroider a pin-cushion or stitch beads on to a purse. Sometimes Papa received a pair of embroidered slippers. Whether he appreciated them we don't know!

Scientific toys were enormously popular during this period. Parents approved of them because they were instructive. There were steam trains which had a brass boiler into which water was poured, to be heated underneath by a methylated spirit stove. There were also replicas of such instruments as the magic lantern, zoetrope, and microscope.

Preparing for a 'charade', or amateur play.

A magic lantern show.

A magic lantern caused great excitement. A sheet was strung across the room as a screen, all the lights were dimmed and only the oil lamp in the lantern glowed. Suddenly before the excited gaze of the assembled family, vivid pictures appeared 'as if by magic' on the screen.

A zoetrope.

The zoetrope, or Wheel of Life, produced an early form of moving picture. When the strip of figures, each in a slightly different position, was viewed through the slots in the rotating cylinder, the figures seemed to be actually moving.

Reading was a favourite pastime with older boys and girls. Many books written in Victoria's reign are still enjoyed today. You may have read some of them. Boys still read the adventure stories of Captain Marryat, G. A. Henty, Mayne Reid, or R. M. Ballantyne. *Tom Brown's Schooldays* is another boys' book from the Victorian period which is still popular.

For girls, the choice was mainly between fairy tales and stories about family life.

'*Miserable* coward,' said Mr. Rose, throwing into the word such ringing scorn that no one who heard it ever forgot it. He indignantly shook the boy off, and caned him till he rolled on the floor, losing every particle of self-control, and calling out, 'The devil —the devil—the devil!' ('invoking his patron saint,' as Wildney maliciously observed).

'There! cease to blaspheme, and get up,' said the master, blowing out a cloud of fiery indignation. 'There, sir. Retribution comes at last, leaden-footed but iron-handed. A long catalogue of sins is visited on you to

Part of a page from Eric, or Little by Little, *a Victorian best-seller.*

The Water Babies by Charles Kingsley, *Alice's Adventures in Wonderland* by Lewis Carroll, *Black Beauty* by Anna Sewell, and *Treasure Island* by Robert Louis Stevenson were all written during Queen Victoria's reign.

The novels of Charles Dickens were enjoyed by the whole family. Often they were read aloud in the evenings when the family were gathered together in the parlour, eager to hear the next instalment in the life of such characters as Oliver Twist or David Copperfield.

Parents did not really approve of comics, and there were not so many in those days. But older children did have magazines like *The Boys' Own Paper*, *The Girls' Own Paper* or *Little Folks*, three of the best known.

A game of marbles, 1860.

OUTDOOR GAMES AND ENTERTAINMENT

Outdoor games changed according to the season, but at different times of the year children played with balls, hoops (either genteel wooden ones or 'common' iron ones) or tops.

Marbles (or *alleys*) was one of the most popular street games. At first alleys were made of clay, but later they were made of a striped stone called agate. In some the stripes were red in colour, and these got the nickname *blood alleys*. Brown ones were called *taws* and the clay ones became known as *commoneys* or *stonies*. Glass marbles out of the necks of bottles were also prized and got the name of *glassies*.

'DIABOLO? OH, YES! IT'S EASY ENOUGH. NO NEED TO WATCH THE THING! NOW, YOU SEE ME TOSS IT UP....'

Diabolo.

Football had been played for centuries in the streets and in the countryside, but it was a rough game and not much like the game we know. The public schools such as Rugby and Eton were the first to start organising the game and laying down rules, about 1850. These rules differed from school to school, especially on the question of whether or not the ball should be handled.

Football at Kingston-upon-Thames, 1864.

The earliest football club was founded in Sheffield in 1855 by Old Boys of the public schools. The Football Association was formed in 1863 and definite rules were laid down. Those who did not agree with the new rules founded the Rugby Union.

Boys playing cricket in the 1840s.

But football in those days was not England's national sport. Cricket was more popular. The village cricket match was an important part of village life. Both fathers and sons practised hard at their bowling and batting, with sisters helping to field. The mother of the great cricketer W. G. Grace used to bowl to her sons in their orchard in Gloucestershire and their dogs were trained to field the ball.

Children who lived in the countryside would also have the pleasures of climbing trees, birds' nesting and angling. In the winter they sometimes went hunting and skating.

For 'young ladies' in towns there were not many outside activities. Archery was considered suitable, and so was a game called croquet. This game was all the rage in the 1860s. It was played on the lawn with a long mallet which was used to knock a ball through a series of hoops. In the 1870s the more familiar (and more energetic) game of tennis took over as the most popular garden game.

There were many street entertainers in Victorian times. German bands (which were brass bands), Scottish bagpipe players and dancers and Italian barrel organ grinders livened up the street with their music.

As you see, for many children, life was far from dull.

Archery.

An organ grinder.

Holidays

ntil 1871 when Bank Holidays were established, there were no official holidays. Country people sometimes took a day off without pay on May Day or on Fair Days, but in the towns most people could not afford to take time off work.

In England an Act of 1871 added Easter Monday, Whit Monday, the first Monday in August and Boxing Day to the traditional holidays of Christmas Day and Good Friday. On those days grown-ups forgot how hard they worked for the rest of the year and made sure that they, and their children, really enjoyed themselves.

THE SEA-SIDE

The most important event of the year for many Victorian families was their annual visit to the sea-side. They planned and saved up for it weeks ahead, whether it was for a month's stay, or just a day trip.

1877.

The rich stayed at 'watering places' such as Weymouth and Brighton in the eighteenth century, but in Victoria's reign the middle classes and working classes also began to visit the sea-side. The new railways made it possible for people to travel there cheaply and easily.

At the height of the summer season the beaches of the popular resorts were so crowded that in places there was hardly any sand to be seen; the streets were thronged with sightseers and shoppers, and there was not a vacant bed to be found in any of the lodging houses.

Even if you were lucky enough to find a bed, the chances were that it was already occupied—by one of the sea-side bugs which were common in those days:

> I am a Bug, a seaside Bug,
> When folks in bed are lying snug,
> About their skin we crawl and creep,
> And feast upon them while they sleep,
> In lodging-houses, where we breed,
> And at this season largely feed.

Crowded beach, 1873.

A visit to the photographer was an important part of the holiday.

Returning from a sail, Brighton, 1884. Notice the sailor suit.

Margate, Ramsgate, Brighton and Bexhill were within easy reach of Londoners and families from the south-east. Blackpool was just developing as a resort for workers in the Lancashire cotton towns, and for Yorkshire people there was Scarborough.

Families who wanted a quiet and fashionable holiday away from the crowds went to the Isle of Wight where the Queen herself had a house.

The middle class families often used to spend a month, or even two, by the sea in summer. They took their servants and rented a house on the seafront to accommodate their large household.

Most working class people never moved far from their own town or village because they could afford neither the time nor the money. But towards the end of the century some working class families were visiting the sea, mainly on day excursion trains. Some of the railway companies made these visits possible by advertising family tickets at a reduced fare.

Day-trippers would travel to the seaside well prepared. In those days there were no cafés or snack bars, and only the rich ate in restaurants, so the trippers would take a huge hamper of food. There would be meat pies and buns, with bottles of beer, tea or lemonade to wash them down. They would also take piles of rugs, shawls, umbrellas, parasols and sun hats.

Day trippers on a steamer.

A donkey ride at Margate.

The charabanc was pulled along at a gentle pace by two, or sometimes three, horses and, in sunny weather, it sported an awning to protect passengers. See also page 32.

On the beach children, as well as adults, usually wore their normal every-day clothes, though the boys might be allowed to roll up their trousers to paddle. Children were never allowed to play on the beach without a cap, hat or bonnet on their head in case they got sun-stroke!

For children, the pleasures of visiting the sea-side have not changed much. There were donkey rides along the sands and Punch and Judy shows at most resorts.

There was also the fascination of searching the rocks for seaweed and shells which could be used to decorate boxes and the edges of mirrors when they returned home. Sometimes they might take a trip in a rowing or sailing boat.

There were also rides in a 'gee-gee cart' or 'charabanc' which was a large wagon with one or two decks and wooden benches.

The pier was a big attraction for children, with its side-shows, slot machines and concert hall. At the concert hall there was often a troupe of entertainers called nigger minstrels who wore straw hats, and striped blazers and blackened faces. They had originated in America but became very popular in England.

One thing you would have found very different in the Victorian period was that men and women bathers were not allowed to mix together on the beach. The Victorians were very modest about certain things, and bathing was one of them. Men and women had their own strip of beach for bathing and must not stray from it.

Ladies' bathing costumes

There was no undressing behind a bath towel in those days. People changed into their swimming costumes and were taken down to the very edge of the sea in a hut-shaped vehicle called a bathing machine. The bathing machine was pulled down the beach by a slow, even-tempered old horse who waited patiently for the bathing to end and then pulled it back up again.

Having gone to all that trouble to bathe, they didn't always enjoy themselves once they were in the sea. Many people bathed simply because they believed it was good for their health. They hired a 'dipper' who was a big, powerful woman. Her job was to seize hold of the bathers as they appeared from the bathing machines and forcibly duck them under the water—several times!

The family Christmas.

CHRISTMAS

Christmas has always been a time for festivity and carol singing, but the Victorians made it more a family celebration than it was before.

The royal family set an example by spending their Christmases together at Windsor. It was there that Prince Albert first introduced the custom of the lighted Christmas tree which he brought from his native Germany. The fir tree, lit by dozens of little coloured wax candles and surrounded by gifts, quickly became one of the best loved symbols of Christmas.

Christmas card, 1872.

The warmth and cheerfulness of the middle class Victorian family Christmas, with rosy faced children and women in crinolines, is often shown in scenes on our modern Christmas cards. But did you know that the custom of wishing friends a merry Christmas in this way first became really popular in the 1870s when cards like the one you see here were sent?

Presents were an important part of Christmas for the well-to-do children. It was the Victorians who first began the custom of hanging their stockings on the bed post on Christmas Eve. For them there was also the fun of children's parties. Their parties were usually large and boisterous with dozens of excited children rushing about playing hunt-the-slipper and musical chairs.

In some villages a team of amateur actors called Mummers visited the manor house and farm houses wearing strange costumes and make-up. They would act a play about St. George and the Turkish Knight. Everyone knew the play, but they never grew tired of seeing it again, and a visit from the Mummers was one of the big excitements of Christmas.

A visit from the Mummers.

Derby Day.

SPECIAL OCCASIONS

Derby Day was a day of special importance for the lower and middle class families of London. Children and grown-ups would rise early and join the huge cheerful crowds making their way on foot, in donkey carts, carriages and all sorts of strange conveyances in the direction of Epsom Downs.

Children of all ages took a great interest in the race itself. They discussed the horses, the riders and the betting as knowledgeably as the grown-ups.

The Downs surrounding the course were great fun for children; there were sideshows with all sorts of freaks, such as the fat lady and the two-headed calf. There were acrobats, jugglers and strong-man acts, gypsy fortune-tellers and rogues who tricked the public with cards and 'thimble-rigging'.

The Oxford and Cambridge Boat Race on the River Thames was another important yearly event in the life of London children. It attracted huge cheering crowds who lined the river along the entire course, wearing pale blue or dark blue ribbons. Some of the little street arabs would hold the spectators' horses for a penny, or would climb trees or dangle precariously from bridges to get a better view.

The Boat Race in 1863. Oxford won and immediately sank. A huge crowd is watching on the far bank.

In many villages the two chief events of the year were the Club Walk and the Wakes. The Clubs (formed to help the sick and unemployed) marched in procession to the parish church carrying white rods, banners and posies. After a service in the church there were games, feasting and dancing.

The Wakes was a time of festivity when families would try to be reunited and friends would visit each other. In the village they set up sideshows and travelling salesmen arrived selling ribbons, trinkets and cheap toys. The whole village joined in contests such as wrestling, climbing a greasy pole to win a pig, or horse-racing.

The Sunday Schools held an annual outing for their pupils, usually at Whitsuntide. They were taken by train or wagon into the countryside or to the seaside where they spent the day eating mountains of sandwiches, drinking gallons of lemonade, playing games and competitions and running races. For many children this would be their one big outing in the whole year.

The greasy pole.

Off to the country.

Working Children

A little more than a hundred years ago, men worked harder and for far longer hours than they do today. Some received a decent wage; others did not. For some men wages were so low that no matter how hard they worked, they could not provide their wife and children with enough food and clothing.

Whether they wanted to or not, such men would be forced to send their children out to work as soon as they were old enough to crawl under machines to clean them, to run errands, to scare crows or to pick up stones in the fields.

Receiving wages after a week's work in the brickyard.

Sometimes the children started work as young as four or five years of age. A young child could not earn much, but even a few pence would be enough in those days to buy his food and prevent him from starving.

For children of poor parents, life was extremely hard. They did not go to school, except perhaps on Sunday; they had no time to play and, through working so hard without nourishing food or fresh air, they mostly grew up weak and sickly.

But there was no shortage of work. Mill owners and other employers were glad to employ children because they did not have to pay them as much as men.

A market for hiring children, 1850.

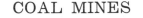

COAL MINES

Nowadays if your parents told you you must go to work down a coal mine where you would be alone in the pitch dark for twelve hours a day, you would think they were inventing tortures to scare you. In the early years of Victoria's reign they would have meant it!

The coal mines of the West Riding of Yorkshire, of Lancashire and east Scotland were dangerous places where roofs sometimes caved in, explosions occurred, and workers suffered all sorts of serious injuries. There were few safety regulations. The heavy work of cutting and moving coal, done nowadays by machines such as conveyor belts, was then done by men, women and children.

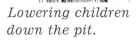

Lowering children down the pit.

Into those dreadful conditions, children were sent to work at an average age of eight or nine, though some started as young as four.

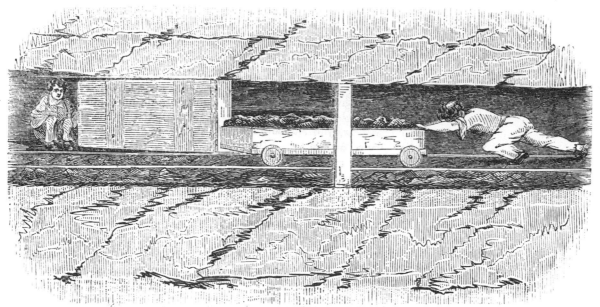

A trapper opening a door for a truck or 'corve' to pass.

The younger children often worked as 'trappers', which means that they operated trap doors. Trappers sat in a hole hollowed out for them and held in their hands a string which was attached to the door. When they heard the coal wagons coming they had to open the door by pulling the string.

This was one of the simplest jobs down the mine and did not require much strength, but it was also one of the loneliest jobs and the place where the child sat was often damp and draughty. It must have been like spending twelve hours a day in a dungeon.

John Saville, seven years old and a collier's boy at the Soap Pit in Sheffield, explained what the job was like for him:

I stand and open and shut the door; I'm generally in the dark, and sit me down against the door; I stop 12 hours in the pit; I never see daylight now, except on Sundays; I fell asleep one day, and a corve ran over my leg and made it smart.

One dreadful job was done by older children, mainly girls. They were employed with women as coal-bearers, carrying loads of coal on their backs in big baskets.

A girl called Ellison Jack, aged eleven, described the work of a coal-bearer:

Coal-bearers climbing a trap.

> I have been working below 3 years on my father's account. He takes me down at 2 in the morning, and I come up at 1 or 2 next afternoon. I go to bed at 6 at night to be ready for work next morning. I have to bear my burthen up 4 traps, or ladders, before I get to the main road which leads to the pit bottom. My task is 4 to 5 tubs, each holding $4\frac{1}{4}$ cwt. I fill 5 tubs in 20 journeys. I have had the strap when I did not do my bidding.

After reading a report about coal mines in 1842, the government passed a Mines Act forbidding the employment of women and girls, and all boys under the age of ten, down mines. Later it became illegal for a boy under the age of 12 to work down a mine, so that half way through Victoria's reign, the cruel slavery of children below ground had ceased.

A mill, illustrated in a novel of 1839.

MILLS

While thousands of children at the start of the reign were toiling down coal mines, thousands of others spent long, monotonous hours crouched over machinery in the cotton mills of Lancashire.

Parishes in those days were supposed to support orphans, but they found this very costly so they preferred to let the mill owners have them. The orphans lived at the mill. Usually the mill owner worked them as hard as he could.

They spent all their waking hours at the machines with no time for fresh air or exercise. Even on Sundays the children had to spend part of the day cleaning the machines.

Serious accidents could occur if the children were not careful. There were cases of children being scalped when their hair was caught in the machine, of hands being crushed, and of children being killed when they went to sleep and fell into the machine.

By 1868, half way through the reign, conditions had improved for mill children too. They were by then being enrolled at the mills as 'short-timers' at the age of eight.

FACTORIES AND
BRICK WORKS

In match factories, children were employed to dip matches into phosphorus. The phosphorus often caused their teeth, and sometimes their entire jaw bone, to rot. Some died from the effect of breathing it into their lungs.

Up and down the country in all sorts of other industries, children were employed. For instance, children were to be found in the potteries of Staffordshire, in the button, glass, and nail-making industries of the Black Country, and in the steel mills of the north.

They were often employed on the heaviest tasks in these heavy industries, as we can see from a report on a girl of twelve in a brick works. This girl formed one of a line who were throwing bricks from one to another. In a day she caught and tossed to her neighbour more than thirty-six tons of bricks!

Working a bellows. Wage, three-pence a day.

She often worked from five in the morning until eight in the evening with only an hour's rest for dinner.

THE CLIMBING BOY

THE SWEEPS' HOME.

[*From a Sketch taken on the Spot.*]

The young sweeps ate and slept in their grime.

The climbing boy, or little chimney sweep, was one of the most pitiful child workers of the nineteenth century. Although in 1832 the use of boys for sweeping chimneys had been forbidden by law, boys continued to be forced through the narrow, winding passages of chimneys in large houses.

Children who became sweeps were those whose parents were either very poor or who did not care very much about them. It is said that sometimes they were stolen from their parents by master sweeps, and even that their parents sold them.

When they first started, at between five and ten years old, the children suffered many grazes, cuts and bruises on their knees, elbows and thighs. After months of suffering, their flesh became hardened enough to withstand such wounds.

If a child showed he was afraid to climb a chimney his master would often 'encourage' him with beatings, knife pricks on his bare soles, or would even light a fire under him!

There were often no facilities for washing, so the sweeps ate with the soot still on their hands and faces and slept in the same clothes they had worn up the chimneys.

Nothing more was done to help the chimney sweep until the 1870s when a man called Lord Shaftesbury brought the government's attention to the death of two sweeps. At last the government promised to make sure people obeyed the law and stopped sending children up chimneys.

STREET CHILDREN

Children in the mines and factories, and even the little chimney sweep, earned a regular wage, even though it wasn't very much. They usually had somewhere to sleep at night. But hordes of dirty, ragged children roamed the streets with no regular money and no home to go to.

Waifs found in the street. The engraving was drawn by Doré, a French artist who was horrified at the poverty he saw in London.

The children of the streets were often orphans. With no-one to care for them, they stole or picked pockets to buy food and slept in outhouses or doorways. Some days they stole nothing and starved. You may have heard of the Artful Dodger in Charles Dickens' *Oliver Twist* who was a pickpocket like these children.

Some of the street children did jobs to earn money instead of stealing it. Some worked as crossing-sweepers, sweeping a way through the mud and horse dung of the main thoroughfares for ladies and gentlemen wishing to cross. Others sold lace, flowers, or muffins, or held the bridles of waiting horses for a penny.

Making a living by selling matches.

Caught by the law.

The street was home for these boys.

COUNTRY CHILDREN

In the countryside too the poor were forced to send their children out to work. Boys at the age of seven or eight became bird scarers, out in the fields in all weathers, from four in the morning until seven in the evening. Older ones worked in gangs with men and women as casual labourers on farms. At least they had the benefit of fresh air.

Country children who worked very much in the same conditions as the factory children of the towns, were those who plaited straw for making into hats. They either did this job at home or in 'schools' which were simply small rooms in the cottages where a lot of children were gathered together to plait under the charge of a mistress. Like the factory children, they were cut off from air and exercise.

A 'gang' of children, hired out to a farmer to work the fields.

By 1876 the government had seen the need to protect country children too. No child under the age of ten could be employed on the land, except at harvest time.

It took time for the government to decide that working children ought to be protected by laws because in those days many people did not see anything wrong

in the idea of children working hard for their keep.

They believed that people should be left alone to help themselves and not expect the government to protect them. They also believed that parents had a right to send their children out to work if they wanted to.

The fact that laws were passed which gradually improved conditions was due to the kindness of such men as Lord Shaftesbury and Sir Robert Peel. They worked hard to persuade the public that it was wrong for children to have their health ruined and be deprived of schooling so that they grew up ignorant and unable to better themselves.

Children born in a slum like this had no chance of education. They would probably live in slums for the rest of their lives.

Children at School

any children in early Victorian England never went to school at all and more than half of them grew up unable even to read or write. There was no law in those days to insist that children went to school, and since all schooling had to be paid for, many parents decided they could not afford the few pence a week it cost to send them.

Other parents managed to send them to school for a year or two, but as soon as they were big enough to do a job, they were sent out to work instead. Very few children ever stayed at school after they were twelve years old.

WORKING CLASS CHILDREN

Some children went to schools built by the Churches, called National Schools and British Schools. They had only one large classroom where pupils of all ages worked together. There might be as many as a hundred pupils in that one room and only one teacher, so his job was very difficult.

Scottish boys walking to school. The boy with the horn called other boys to join them.

He would sit at a high desk and keep order by dealing out canings for the smallest faults. You would have found him very strict indeed. Older pupils called *monitors* helped him by teaching the younger children to read in small groups. Monitors had to stay behind after school to be taught their own lessons for the next day.

The school itself was a grim building. The classroom was warmed only by a single stove or an open fire, and there were no attractive books to read or interesting apparatus to use. The children were taught only to read, write, do sums and mental arithmetic and Scripture; the girls sometimes learned to knit and sew.

But the children who attended the Church Schools were better taught than many who attended Dame Schools.

A ragged school, for the very poor.

A Dame School—most were not as good as this.

These were run by old ladies, who taught in their front parlour, where often they had no proper seats, desks, or books. At a particularly bad Dame School a government Inspector found:

> ... 31 children, from 2 to 7 years of age. The room was a cellar about 10 feet square and about 7 feet high. The only window was less than 18 inches square and not made to open. Here they sat totally destitute of books. The only remaining instruments of instruction possessed by the dame, were a glass-full of sugar-plums and a cane by its side.

Many children already at work found their only chance to learn anything was on a Sunday at the Church or Chapel Sunday School.

To attend a Sunday School children had to be clean and tidily dressed, but some children were so filthy and shabby that the teachers turned them away. A new sort of school called a 'ragged school' was set up for them. Orphans, beggars, crossing sweepers and children nobody cared about went to the ragged schools.

Rugby at Rugby School

BETTER-OFF BOYS

Rich boys were taught either at home in the school-room by a private tutor or were sent to a public school such as Eton, Harrow, Winchester or Rugby. They were taught very little except Latin and Greek, which must have been very boring.

At a public school in the earlier part of the century a boy might have had a hard time, because they were rough places. There was fighting, bullying and even rioting, when the school had to be closed down and the police sent for.

Yet, by the middle of the century, public schools had improved a good deal and had become very popular with parents. The improvement was largely due to one man— Thomas Arnold, who became headmaster of Rugby in 1827. He aimed to turn the boys into what he described as 'Christian gentlemen'. To do this he used three methods —discipline, religion and good sportsmanship.

Middle class parents sent their sons to grammar schools which dated back several hundred years to the time of Edward VI and Elizabeth I, or to private boarding schools. In some of the boarding schools the food, dormitories, and teaching were shockingly poor.

Some of the worst schools were in Yorkshire, and they even advertised as one of their attractions, that they didn't give the boys holidays.

Charles Dickens helped to bring an end to the worst type of boarding school by writing a book called *Nicholas Nickleby* which described one called Dotheboys Hall. Its headmaster, Whackford Squeers, exclaimed, 'Let any boy speak a word without leave and I'll take the skin off his back.'

FEBRUARY — Cutting Weather

At least one Victorian schoolmaster flogged a boy to death. Severe punishment was thought good for boys.

Governess and pupils.

BETTER-OFF GIRLS

Wealthy girls were mostly taught at home by their Mama or by a governess, who made sure they did not learn too much, for a well educated girl was often frowned upon in those days. People called her a 'blue-stocking' and said she would never find a husband.

A young lady's education was supposed to train her for marriage, and nothing more. To attract a husband they believed a girl must have some 'accomplishments'. These included sketching, playing the piano, singing and embroidery. Sometimes girls were sent to young ladies' academies, which were boarding schools, for a final polish to their accomplishments.

Victorian girls also practised 'deportment', which is the art of sitting and moving. They walked with straight backs and heads held high, and practised for hours walking round a room balancing a heavy book on their head.

EDUCATION FOR ALL

In 1870 the government finally passed a law that all children between the ages of five and thirteen must go to school and their parents must pay a small amount towards the cost.

At first this law was very unpopular with some of the parents who did not like being forced to send their children to school. Some even tried to trick the authorities by saying their children had died, when really they were out at work.

The numbers of children attending school increased so much there were not enough schools to accommodate them all. New schools had to be built, called Board Schools because they were run by a board of governors. They were ugly, barrack-like buildings, often with bars at the windows and little space for playgrounds, but the children were taught by trained teachers and in a bigger variety of subjects which included History, Geography and P.E. (known as 'drill').

An Infant Board School. Notice the child on the left in the front row.

Family Life

For the middle classes, Victoria's reign was a happy and prosperous time. Families were often large. It was common to have eight or ten children. Houses too were large, with many servants to run them, and were full of life and activity, especially when all the children were home from school.

Papa was head of this large household and took his position seriously. He was very stern and strict compared with fathers today, but perhaps he had to be, with so many servants and children to keep in order. When he wanted a little peace and quiet he retired into his study and the rest of the household were not allowed to enter without his special permission.

The children respected Papa and always spoke politely to him, addressing him as 'Sir'. Very few children would have dared be cheeky to their father or answer him back, and he rarely discussed his work or other business with them, for those were grown-up matters and not the concern of children.

Papa as he liked to be seen.

Morning prayers were quite normal in many families—but this is an idealised picture.

Mama often left the care of her children to the servants and spent her time planning dinner parties, visiting her dress-maker, or calling on friends. But although she did not do jobs such as washing their clothes or cooking their meals, she sometimes taught the younger children to read and write, and she made sure that all her children were well brought up.

Both Papa and Mama saw the upbringing of their children as an important responsibility. They believed a child must be taught the difference between right and wrong if he was to grow into a good and thoughtful adult.

If a child did something wrong he would be punished, for his own good. 'Spare the rod and spoil the child' was a saying the Victorians firmly believed in. Telling lies or disobedience were serious offences for which children would be caned.

For less serious offences such as squabbling, or arriving late for a meal, the unfortunate culprit might be sent to bed with no supper, have his toys taken away, or be stood face to the wall in a corner.

But despite such punishments most adults remembered their childhood as a happy time, full of amusement and interesting happenings. Children did not creep about in fear and dread of punishment, they accepted it as part of life and did not make a fuss or bear resentment. The majority of them grew into sympathetic, hardworking adults.

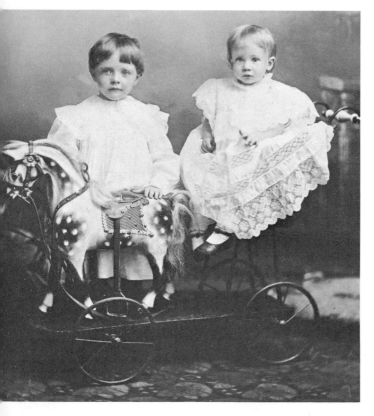

Most days middle class children saw very little of their parents, for they spent much of their time in the nursery. There the younger ones played with their toys, invented their own mysterious family games, and made a lot of noise. In charge of the nursery was Nanny, with sometimes a nursemaid, or even two to help her.

In the nursery.

Children being shown off to their parents' guests before dinner.
Nanny carries the baby.

Victorian children were expected to rise early, because lying in bed was thought to be lazy and sinful. In some households they were expected to get up and practise the piano for half an hour before breakfast.

Lunch was the main meal for children, and sometimes the older ones had to eat it with their Mama and her guests to get them used to company. It could be quite an ordeal for the shy and clumsy ones, who had to be on their best behaviour, remembering their table manners, swallowing their food without speaking, and not daring to choke over a fish bone or drop a fork, because that would mean the instant disgrace of being sent from the table or refused any pudding!

Sometimes, on the evenings when there were no guests, the children would go down to the richly furnished drawing room to join their parents for an hour or so. There they had to behave with 'decorum' in order not to knock over Mama's many ornaments and 'knick-knacks', so they would take something they could do quietly such as embroidery or reading.

Occasionally, they would take turns with their parents to read aloud from a book the whole family could enjoy, such as *The Water Babies* or a novel by Charles Dickens. If they were a musical family, those with passably good voices might be invited to sing or others would play the piano.

One of the attractions of the drawing room was its large warm fire. Elsewhere, the house was rather cold and draughty, for there was no central heating in those days. The children were not 'pampered' with heating in their rooms unless they were ill or taking a bath.

Family group in the 1890s.

Middle class boys in sailor suits, playing with a toy cannon.

Bathrooms were rare before the turn of the century, so children, and adults too, bathed in a tin bath called a 'hip bath' which was usually placed on towels before the bedroom fire. Servants had the difficult job of staggering up several flights of stairs with large jugs of water to fill the bath.

Because middle class children formed part of a close-knit family group which they rarely left, they were protected from the worries and troubles of the outside world. In some ways this was good, because they grew up feeling loved and secure. But it also meant that they did not come into contact with children who were less fortunate than themselves, and perhaps did not fully understand the troubles and problems of the poor.

The better-off working class families on the whole were as close and devoted to each other as the middle class families were, but in their smaller houses with no servants to help them, a really big family could have its problems. No matter how fond brothers were of each other, they probably found that sleeping three or four to a bed, as many did, caused short tempers as they grew older.

Mother had to work really hard to feed her family and keep them neat and tidy, for she had no modern aids such as washing machines, electric irons, or pre-packaged foods. Even so, the family generally managed to have a comfortable life with enough to eat and a little money to spare for holidays and entertainment.

Farm worker's home, 1872.

For the lesser-paid families the great fear was the workhouse, where thousands of homeless and penniless families were forced to live.

Male ward at the workhouse.

Charlie Chaplin, the great star of silent films, remembers in his autobiography the shame of moving with his mother and brother from a comfortable flat into only two rooms, then only one room, and finally into a workhouse, where he and his brother were separated from their mother and only allowed to see her at appointed times in an interview room. They were dressed in workhouse clothes and had their hair cropped short.

Every poor family lived in dread of being split up like this in a workhouse and having to spend the rest of their life there. It could happen quite easily if father were taken ill suddenly and could not work.

Even families who lived in a cellar, or shared one room or a tumble-down cottage with another family were better off than those in a workhouse. Despite their miseries, they were at least together.

In slums like this (1889) disease and death could not be avoided.

But children born into poor homes could count themselves lucky to be alive at all. Many would have known brothers and sisters who had died. Nowadays the death of a baby or a young child is unusual, but in those days even wealthy parents knew that some of their children might die before they were five years old.

Children died of diseases for which medical science had then found no cure. The diseases were spread by foul drinking water, open drains and lack of proper washing and toilet facilities, as well as air polluted by smoke. In the overcrowded rooms of the poor if one person caught a disease it spread quickly to the rest. Scarlet fever, measles, polio or tuberculosis, which are now understood and are rarely serious, were often fatal.

Many poor children died as a result of the cold, damp conditions they lived in, or through lack of good food. Others grew up weak and sickly with diseases such as rickets, which weakened their legs and spine.

THE VICTORIAN SUNDAY

Most Victorian families were 'God-fearing'. Each day Papa would take the family prayers when the whole household, including the servants would kneel and pray.

In the later part of the reign especially they were very strict about keeping the whole of Sunday as a day of rest and prayer. All shops were closed and there was no sport or amusement.

Some families would go to church twice, to both the morning and evening service. The family, led by Papa, would troop into church wearing their best clothes and sit in the family pew. The sermons were often long and boring for the children, but they were not supposed to fidget or to show that their attention was wandering.

In the afternoon, between church services, some were sent for a third helping of religion at Sunday School. Others accompanied their parents on a walk or a visit to neighbours.

If they stayed at home they were not allowed to play games or read story books. All toys were locked away and the only sort of books they could read were religious ones—the Bible or Foxe's Book of Martyrs. Hymn singing round the piano was one of the few things into which they could put some life and energy.

Hymn-singing.

But Sunday, trying as it was, was only one day out of the whole week, and doubtless children dispelled some of the gloom by dreaming up new games and adventures to fill the other six.

The life of a Victorian child was certainly different in many ways from the life of children now, but was not completely different. There are certain 'timeless' things that children will perhaps always enjoy and do.

This kind of poverty is no longer widespread.

Nowadays changes and inventions have altered life a lot, and many of them have made it better; poverty in England is no longer widespread, and all children have the chance of a good education.

But whether or not all children now are happier than they were in Victoria's reign it is impossible to say. Then they were satisfied with a little, now most are satisfied only with a lot, but are they better satisfied?

But how much have people themselves changed?

Other Books

Everyday Things in England (volumes 3 & 4) by M. & C. H. B. Quennell (Batsford)

English Children's Costume since 1775 by I. Brooke (Black)

Period Piece by G. Raverat (Faber)

Life in Victorian England by W. J. Reader (Batsford)

At School and in the Country in 1900 by Sallie Purkiss and Elizabeth Merson (Longman)

The Victorian Age by Peter Lane (Batsford)

Two Victorian Families by Sue Wagstaff (A & C Black)

INTERESTING PLACES TO VISIT

Bath, The Assembly Rooms (Costume)

Cambridge, The Folk Museum

Edinburgh, The Museum of Childhood

Rugeley, Staffs, Museum of Childhood and Costume, Blithfield Hall

London, The Victoria & Albert Museum, South Kensington

London, Bethnal Green Museum

Warwick, Doll Museum

York, Castle Museum and The Debtors' Prison

Many other museums have exhibits from the Victorian period.

A girl in the 1870s, wearing button boots and a bustle.

Index